Enjoy a bit of Nonsense!

Dennis Rodgers

A Little Bit of
Nonsense
A Wacky Poetry Collection

A Little Bit of
Nonsense

A Wacky Poetry Collection
by
Denise Rodgers

Illustrated by Julie Martin

Published by Creative Writing Press, Inc., 3642 West Eleven Mile Road,
Berkley, Michigan 48072.

Printed in the United States of America.

Publisher's Cataloging-in-Publication
(Provided by Quality Books, Inc.)

Rodgers, Denise
    A little bit of nonsense : a wacky poetry collection
/ by Denise Rodgers ; illustrated by Julie Martin. --
1st ed.
    p. cm.
    Includes index.
    Audience: Grades K-6.
    LCCN 2001087860
    ISBN 0-9708382-0-4

    1. Children's poetry, American. [1. American poetry.]
I. Martin, Julie, 1955- II. Title.

PS3535.0332Li 2001   811'.6
        QBI01-700511

Table of Contents

I. Characters I Have Known

A Little Bit of Nonsense 2

Herbert Hillbert Hubert Snod 4

My Uncle Jack 5

Lucia Hemphill Todd McBean 6

Slicing Salami 8

Matthew Brindle, Upside Down 9

Grandpa Used to Shave Each Day 10

Aunt Myrtle Has Geraniums 12

Stacking Dishes 14

Lazy Jane 15

Betty's Room 16

Marrying Margaret 18

The Old Woman and the Magical Sack 19

His Look Is Wild 20

Sudden Baldness 21

Silly Sally 21

Henry the Hatter 22

Matthew McHavish 24

A Garden More Than Odd 26

Rapunzel 28

II. Monster-Meat Stew (and other delicacies)

Monster-Meat Stew 30

Never Ask a Cow to Dine 31

Crack an Egg 32

Moon Eggs 33

My Gramma Can't Bake Cookies 34

Famished Famella 35

Melon Head 36

Handy Storage 37

Tasteful Jewelry 38

Creamed Spinach Soufflé 39

Jelly, Jam, and Buttered Toast 40

Cranberry Sauce 41

Take a Poem to Lunch 42

III. Noah's Ark

Noah's Ark 44
Undercover Raccoon 45
The Hippo 46
Eloise 47
The Shark 48
The Dogfish Really Is a Shark 49
Underbite 50
Goose and Moose 51
Nervous Rex 52
If Dogs Could Talk 53
Aunt Jane's Cats 54
The Curiosity Shop 55
Snail Races 56
Slithery, Slidery, Scaly Old Snake 57
The Elephant Has a Bad Earache 58

IV. Loony Ideas

Questions 60
I Wish 62
The Wild Calliope 63
A Note to the Moth Who Ate My Sweater 64
Odd Pets 65
Shampoo, Shampoo 66
Spinning Dry 67
The Nose 68
My Leaky Faucet 69
The Wind Was Wild 70
The Sun Just Had a Nasty Day 71
Pillow Soft, Pillow Deep 72
If Dinosaurs Once More Could Roam 73
Cyclops 74
There's Something Growing in Our House 75
Mining for a Poem 76
I Work with Words 77
Counting Sheep 78

Title Index 80

Acknowledgments

There is a certain irony about the number of people involved in the creation of a book — after the solitary pursuit of writing it. I'd like to thank Julie Martin, an artist and illustrator who has been a joy to both work — and rub creative elbows — with. To Shelley Lazarus, an exceptional writing buddy and friend who convinced me that this project was possible, and who gave me an opportunity to visit with the wonderful students of Pine Lake Elementary School. To Kevin Kammeraad and Jane Stroschin, for their personal and professional encouragement and advice. To Amy Marcaccio Keyzer for her enthusiastic and insightful job of copyediting the manuscript that was to become this book (and for teaching me the difference between a verso and a recto). To Ann Little, for years of being an honest critic and friend. To Joan Brode and Florence Steinberg, my coffee-time poetry friends. To Gayle Bialick, for helping in the final proof-reading stage. To Brian DePoy for the patience of a saint and the wisdom of a MacMaster (and also because it is tremendous good luck for Michigan publishers to thank him in their books). To Doug Alden Peterson, of Visualeyes, who matches Brian in the infinite patience department, for his creative expertise on ThePoetryLady.com web site and for his input and help with the creation of this book cover. To Southfield Public Library's children's librarians Char Watch and Cindy Cares for their interest and help with this project. To Jack Prelutsky, who gave me the thrill of a lifetime by including "Slicing Salami" in his anthology. To my sister, Flora Zack, who has always believed in me as a writer, and who not so incidentally introduced my work to Jack, and who brought me to Dallas for my first elementary school visit. To Ted, who sees the world from a unique slant and who has given me years of material. To David, who taught me how to hear (and count) the music in my poetry. To Roselie and George Ohrenstein, my mom and dad, for reading to me and Flora when we were kids — and keeping wonderful books around the house. And last, and absolutely not least, to Peter, my #1 fan and partner, in business and in life.

Denise Rodgers

I would like to thank Denise Rodgers for the wonderful opportunity to be a part of this book. It's been great fun. Also, thanks to Leon, Lee and Ross for your love and support. With love from Mom.

Julie Martin

I. Characters I Have Known

A Little Bit of Nonsense

A little bit of nonsense starts
each morning, night and noon —
like a twenty-two-foot sundae
with a boat oar for a spoon.
An oversized, tall portly man
who wears a tiny hat.
A mammoth, giant schnauzer
who is frightened of a cat.

A man who goes to work each day
and figures that instead
of sitting he would rather work
while balanced on his head.
A toddler, quite intelligent,
who perches on a stool
and teaches all the college kids
each afternoon at school.

A friendly gray pet dragon who
his master can inspire
to fix a daily supper with
his very handy fire.
A double-wide young hippo,
who's a well-loved family pet,
that crashes through the attic floor,
befuddled and upset.

A temperamental pastry chef,
who's awfully fond of cake.
Just ordering your treats from her
could be a large mistake.
For when depressed, she eats a lot.
It really is my fear
she'll get upset in time to make
your order disappear.

And in the deepest jungle, there's
the least-known people zoo.
The animals come staring to
see what the people do.
The people, bored, in cages,
kind of stand around and scratch
while animals keep waiting
for a baby-man to hatch.

The world is full of quirky stuff,
of acts and things bizarre
from monkeys at the barber's
to a zebra in a car.
But if you cannot see it,
it is not that you are blind.
The nonsense is available;
it's waiting in your mind.

3

Herbert Hillbert Hubert Snod

Herbert Hillbert Hubert Snod
was known for eating all things odd.
The thing that bothered me the most
was he spread toothpaste on his toast.
"It's springtime fresh, so cool and minty."
His smiling eyes were bright and squinty.

On baked potatoes, he would slather
one-half can of shave cream lather.
Who knows how his tum could cope
as he ingested cubes of soap.
At times his food choice made a scene;
at least he kept his innards clean.

4

My Uncle Jack

This poem is a tale about my Uncle Jack
who has hair on his legs, on his arms, on his back,
on his knees, on his hands, hair all over the place.
And if he didn't shave, he'd have hair on his face.

The only place lacking of hair is his head.
He has a white dome of smooth skin there instead.
He peels fresh bananas and eats like Godzilla.
By now you have guessed . . .
He's a piebald gorilla.

Lucia Hemphill Todd McBean

Lucia Hemphill Todd McBean
painted her whole house bright green.
She started with the porch and door,
then dipped her brush and painted more.

She painted every piece of brass,
the porchlight bulb and porchlight glass.
She painted all the trim and brick,
with two thick coats to make it stick.

She painted her whole shingled roof
without a drip or drop or goof.
She stepped back, feeling satisfied
and then began to paint inside.

She painted every floor and wall,
the ceiling beams, but that's not all.
She painted every couch and chair,
the banister and every stair.

She painted every glass and cup
and still the paint was not used up.
So, feeling not quite done, she sat
and painted both her dog and cat.

Before the paint went on the shelf
she painted her entire self.
So now her house is such a scene;
you cannot find her for the green.

But don't feel bad for missing Lucia.
Next year she is painting fuchsia.

Slicing Salami

The strangest strange stranger I've met in my life
was the man who made use of his nose as a knife.
He'd slice up salami, tomatoes and cheese
at the tip of his nose with phenomenal ease.

He'd buy food in bulk at incredible prices
and then use his nose to reduce it to slices.
His wife ran away and I know that he'll miss her.
The woman was frightened that one day he'd kiss her!

Matthew Brindle, Upside Down

Matthew Brindle, bright and strong

has his ups and downs all wrong.

Walks around on his two hands,

making very few demands.

Humble from his airborne toes

right down to his earthbound nose.

Works with head down on his seat.

In the air are his two feet.

Matt's boss said that he's no shirker,

is, in fact, a model worker.

"Always thinks of something new. . .

I guess that's just his point of view."

Grandpa Used to Shave Each Day

Grandpa used to shave each day,
but now he's grown a beard.
It's long and scraggly, gray and white.
I think it's kind of weird.

It used to be a short goatee,
but Grandpa grew it longer.
He says it makes it kind of coarse
and also, much, much stronger.

My grandpa is a kindly man,
and tried his very best,
to say "no" to the robin who
flew in and built a nest
inside his beard, beneath his chin
and now it never fails
that Grandpa's beard is full of nest
and many screws and nails,
a tiny claw-head hammer and
a driver for his screws.
My grandpa's beard holds many tools
that he will never use.

Now Grandma's getting cranky, says
it's hard for her to sleep
with lumpy tools inside their bed
and all that cheep, cheep, cheep.
Besides the screws and nails and tools,
besides the nest and bores,
my grandpa's a sound sleeper with
a tendency to snore.

My grandma wants to strangle him,
but we know how to save her.
Tomorrow is his birthday, and
our dad bought him a shaver.

11

Aunt Myrtle Has Geraniums

Aunt Myrtle has geraniums
around her kitchen sink.
And most are red with bright green leaves,
a few, a darkish pink.

She's Boston ferns, and Chinese jade
and little pots of ivy.
Where other people place one plant,
Aunt Myrtle places five-y.
A giant palm, a cactus patch,
a room of yellow daisies.
Her living room has rows of green
that look just like a maze-y.
At feeding time Aunt Myrtle says
her babies are all thirsty.
She waters up her small green friends
until they want to burst-y.

The water spills and marks and stains
the carpet on the floor.
It never stops Aunt Myrtle, who
will always water more.

When water time is over,
Auntie Myrtle takes a rest
and soaks in a hot bath tub in
her very favorite dress.

She sings a song at naptime till
her planties go to sleep.
She shushes at the doorbell, so
her plants won't hear a peep.

She covers every plant up with
a special, hand-sewn blankey.
She sneezes very softly in
her green and yellow hanky.

She rotates every plant each day
so it may see the sun.
She dances as she rotates, as
she says it's much more fun.
Aunt Myrtle may be crazy, as
by now you sure can tell.
Her dresses might get soggy, but
her plants do very well.

Stacking Dishes

Did you know my cousin, Bree,
said, "Washing dishes? Not for me!"
And so, alas, it is her fate
that she can never find a plate
without some hardened sauce or rice.
There isn't one that's clean and nice.

When she runs out, what can she do?
She goes to shop and buys them new.
But once she's dirtied plate and cup,
she goes ahead and stacks them up.

It doesn't look at all appealing
seeing plates stacked to the ceiling.
I said, "Bree, it's not too late
to go and buy a paper plate."
Said Bree,
"You must think me a pauper!
Paper plates are so improper."

So her dishes block the light.
At least she thinks that she's polite.

14

Lazy Jane

Here's the tale of lazy Jane
who lost the use of half her brain.
She could retrieve it, hasn't yet.
It's right beside her TV set.
She found her programs wild and thrilling.
All the while her brain was spilling
through her ear and on the floor,
as she forgot what it is for.
And so it sits, a pile of gray.
It's useless to this very day.

About her programs, Jane does scoff,
"I've half a mind to turn them off."

Betty's Room

There is no clutter cluttered up
more closely, I presume,
than the clutter clustered clingingly
in my friend, Betty's room.

Her mother mutters mawkishly
and fills her with such dread.
She mutters on about the muss
that messes Betty's bed.

At bedtime, Betty bounces all
her objects to the floor.
Each morning, when she wakes up, they
go on her bed once more.

There's papers, pencils, potpourri.
It piques her mother's stress.
She pouts. She plies and yet her cries
do not clean Betty's mess.

There's partly broken plastic toys,
each with a missing part,
some worn and withered whistles, which
are close to Betty's heart.

Old ballet shoes she cannot lose,
and photos of her friends,
a burnt-out fuse, some fruity chews,
a box of odds and ends.

Old magazines and school reports
(the ones that got the A's),
her worn out jeans, some socks to sort,
the programs from three plays.
Each object is an artifact,
a personal antique.
She cannot bear to throw them out;
they make her life unique.
There's feathers, fans and fairy dolls —
and mother-daughter strife.

Her mother lives for neatness, but, well, mess is Betty's life.

Marrying Margaret

Margaret Merkser-Cooper-Roberts-
Langstrom-Berger-Glen-
Pearson-Smith-MacPherson-Dobb's
on husband number ten.
Merkser was a painter, who
fell off a trellis ladder,
Cooper, a psychologist,
who said it didn't matter.
Roberts, a designer, with
aristocratic flair,
Langstrom was a barber, who
cut all her bright red hair,
Berger, a podiatrist
so fond of lancing corns,
Glen, a simple gardener,
who worked with weeds and thorns.
Pearson was a druggist who
forever counted pills,
Smith, a young physician, who
fought flus and other ills.
Then there was MacPherson
who taught English at the school,
Dobb, a full-time hustler
who is fond of playing pool.
Margaret loves a wedding;
it's her next best thing to heaven.
Already she is searching for
one more to make eleven.

The Old Woman and the Magical Sack

There is an old woman quite gray and quite stooped,
her wrinkles beneath a straw hat quaintly drooped.
Her body is bent from her waist to her back.
Her hand is clasped tight to her magical sack.
This sack, at first glance, seems just simple and usable.
But that's just first glance. Oh, the sack is so musical!

Even when closed, sealed up tight as a drum,
if you listen closely, you hear a soft hum.
If opened a smidgen, in either direction,
her sack gives the sound of a tuning string section.
She opens it wide and how wildly astounding.
Inside is a symphony concert that's sounding
like sunrise in song. It will make your heart stir.

If you walk about town, keep your eye out for her,
with her hat and her sack. But don't ask where she's from.
Just follow her closely and hear the soft hum.

His Look Is Wild

His look is wild.
His name is Fred.
His hair completely hides his head.
Take a peek.
(Show no surprise.)
You cannot even see his eyes.
Oh no, it must be as I feared.
His mouth is covered by his beard.
How does he breathe?
How does he eat?
How does he see to cross the street?
Perhaps he can't see people stare
and cannot find the barber chair.
Until he makes a barber stop
he will remain less man than mop.

Sudden Baldness

"Oh my!" the portly gent called out.
"I cannot find my hair.
I washed and put it out to dry
and now it isn't there!"

Silly Sally

When Silly Sally irons her clothes,
they come out looking awful.
She did not read the label and
her iron was meant to waffle.

21

Henry the Hatter

I'm Henry the Hatter
and what does it matter?
Just what does my name mean to you?
I've quite a selection,
a mammoth collection
of hats. I have much more than few.

I've hats made for swimming,
with bright silver trimming,
a top hat to wear with a cane.
I've helmets for biking,
a beige hat for hiking,
a red hat to wear in the rain.

I've team hats for ball games,
and sport caps with all names.
In case you are feeling selective,
I've beréts for Frenchmen,
and black hoods for henchmen,
and hats that are worn by detectives.

I'm Henry the Hatter.
Excuse while I natter
the only name I'm ever called.
The truth is just that
I am known for my hats
because I am totally bald.

Matthew McHavish

Matthew McHavish was so fond of stuff,
he'd always want more and had never enough
of watches and baskets and buzz saws and toasters,
of pitchers and thick books and modern art posters,
of holiday figures and skates made for ice,
of fine China coasters, computers with mice.

He found his collecting a bit problematic.
He ran out of room in his basement and attic.
He still was not daunted and shopped a bit more.
He bought out his neighbor and moved in next door,
maintaining his first home for storage of things,
of large rolltop desks and of small diamond rings,
of ice chests and freezers to keep some things chilled.
In less than one year, he had two houses filled.

He bought out more neighbors — this may cause a shock —
he set out to buy every house on the block.
In less than a decade (it made him feel giddy),
he bought every house he could find in the city.

Alas, life is short, to our death from our birth.
If Matthew could do it, he'd buy the whole earth.

A Garden More Than Odd

Mary Merksam Maxim Dodd
has a garden more than odd.
She thinks it just a handsome treat
to grow a prickly row of feet.
The next row, shock, to your surprise,
is tender shoots of long-lashed eyes.
It won't at all allay your fears
to see her row of hairy ears.
And right next to her prize-won roses
is a row of sneezing noses.

She sprinkles antihistamine
and wipes the noses dry and clean.

26

Her favorite row, of few demands
is one made up of waving hands.
How does she tend her garden patch?
She enters quick, and draws the latch.
She feeds her "plants" some roast beef lean,
potatoes, mashed, and lima beans.
She grinds it with her handheld mixer,
makes a helpful "plant" elixir.

But I've heard her often gripe,
"What will I do, when they come ripe?"
As some will run off in the breeze,
and some will snap and some will sneeze.
But some will see her hopeful face,
and to her joy, will stay in place.

Rapunzel

Rapunzel got a haircut
as her long hair was a bother.
She wrapped it all around her waist
and went out with her father.
He took her to the barber shop.
The barber's scissors gave a chop.
She asked to make a real close crop.
When it was short, she said to stop.

The prince was quite confounded
when he came again to visit.
"Rapunzel, you look different.
Something's changed. Tell me, what is it?"
He tried to climb the tower, but
he found he wasn't able,
      so fearful that the vines along
       the tower were unstable.

The prince went home unhappy
that his girlfriend was unfair.
He wondered what would cause her to
chop off her useful hair.
She didn't change her address and
she didn't change her name.
Rapunzel got a haircut and
she wasn't quite the same.

Monster-Meat Stew

(and other delicacies)

Monster-Meat Stew

Have you ever feasted on monster-meat stew
washed down with a large mug of Frankenstein's brew,
and served by a waitress, who cackles and chews,
with cheerful green skin and a large wart or two?

Have you ever chowed down on lizard-meat pie,
washed down with a pitcher of water run dry,
and served by a waiter with red-colored eye,
who trips on his pitchfork when he stumbles by?

Have you ever gobbled down buzzard au gratin?
It's best when the cheese that it's cooked with is rotten
and served by a warlock, who's better forgotten,
whose pointy wide ears are both stuffed with white cotton?

I've asked all my questions. Your answer's complete.
Yet, I am confused. Tell me, what *do* you eat?

Never Ask a Cow to Dine

Never ask a cow to dine
on roasted quail or porcupine.
And please don't make the huge mistake
of ordering a T-bone steak
or braised beef tips cooked by the dozen.
(To her it may look like a cousin.)

Just order up the salad fare
and skip the brisket — extra rare.
For extra courses what she needs
is tall, wild grass and common weeds.
But worry not — if food's a dud
your dinner date may chew her cud.
Just watch her as she starts to chew,
and if she talks — you'll hear her moo.

Crack an Egg

Crack an egg.

Stir the butter.

Break the yolk.

Make it flutter.

Stoke the heat.

Hear it sizzle.

Shake the salt,

just a drizzle.

Flip it over,

just like that.

Press it down.

Squeeze it flat.

Pop the toast.

Spread jam thin.

Say the word.

Breakfast's in.

Moon Eggs

Moon eggs, moon eggs.
Mom makes up the moon eggs,
not sunny-side up,
not boiled in a cup,
not fried over easy
(which makes me so queasy),
not scrambled and stirred,
or whipped up and whirred,
but sunny-side down
like a frown on a clown.
The yolk isn't runny
or face up and sunny,
but solid and tasty,
if just a bit pasty.
I'll eat with my spoon
my eggs like the moon.

My Gramma Can't Bake Cookies

My gramma can't bake cookies, and
she's not too good at cakes,
and every time she tries to, she
comes up with new mistakes.
She baked a batch of chocolate chips
and set the heat so high,
the cookies turned to charcoal slabs
that looked like her peach pie.

She tried to bake some cupcakes, but
she could not find a cup.
She tried to make pineapple cake,
and it turned right-side up.
Whenever Gramma frosts a cake,
it splits and kind of breaks.
Thank goodness Gramma likes to take
me out for chocolate shakes.

Famished Famella

I am famously famished Famella.
Strangers stop and they stare while I eat.
I can gobble up seven cheese pizzas
and five layered cakes as a treat.

I am fervently famished Famella.
I can quickly down three loaves of bread
thickly slathered with grape jam and cream cheese,
or sweet apple butter instead.

I'm the fortunate famished Famella.
I can eat any food that I choose —
chocolate tortes, cherry crepes or fresh knockwursts,
they all taste so great, I can't lose.

I'm the faltering famished Famella.
While I have no desire to be rude,
you will have to excuse me this moment,
as I've gone far too long without food.

Melon Head

My best friend is a melon head,
and when it's time to snack instead
of munching on some cheese or toast,
his favorite snack he likes the most
is chunks of melon, piled on bread.
He gets the melon from his head.
I fear that it's become a drain
on his forever shrinking brain.

Handy Storage

He was a short man. As he waddled about,
I counted his chins from his chest to his snout.
His chins were all smooth, neither grizzled nor dirty.
I hadn't stopped counting, when I'd counted thirty!
"Are your chins a nuisance?" I ventured to ask.
He said, "They are not, though it is a great task
just keeping them neat. Yet they come in quite handy
for storing my pencils and notecards and candy."
He lifted chin ten, where the lemon drops stay.
I took one, said, "Thanks!"
He said, "Have a nice day!"

Tasteful Jewelry

There is a stunning woman who
has culinary zeal.
She dresses very casually.
Her jewelry is real.
She's not fond of perfumery.
Take caution when she's near —
she wears two fresh-finned mackerel.
One dangles from each ear.
She slips two bagel bracelets on
her very slender arms.
She nibbles at the poppy seeds
and forms some cream-cheese charms.
Her romaine lettuce pendant has
a pepper as a drop.
Her fingers slide through olives with
pimentos at the top.
Her belt is bright red licorice.
She gives her head a pat.
A pretzel is her hair pin,
chocolate babka is her hat.
There's not a bit of foodstuff that
she'll ever care to waste.
Her style may be peculiar, but
she's always in good taste.

Creamed Spinach Souffle´

My father is making creamed spinach soufflé.
It's going to be a magnificent day.
The spinach is stringy. The creamed glop is white.
It's going to be a magnificent night.
He's heating up stewed beets to serve on the side.
He's chopping and stirring and cooking with pride.
He's picked out a fresh orange and grinding the rind
to place on the beets. See, I really don't mind.
I don't mind the spinach or even the beets. Ahhh!
I'm eating at Jason's and we're having pizza.

Jelly, Jam, and Buttered Toast

Jelly, jam, and buttered toast.
I like breakfast food the most.
Bagels, cream cheese, juice — fresh squeeze,
make me say, pass more here please.

Lunch will often make me mutter.
I'm not fond of peanut butter.
I hate chips that won't go crunch.
Truly, I do not like lunch.

Now dinner is another meal
I'll take or leave, that's how I feel.
There's always veggies I can't stand.
I have to eat them on demand.

If I could choose and have my way,
well, we'd eat breakfast food all day.

Cranberry Sauce

Cranberry sauce,
cranberry sauce.
Yes, I'm at a loss
about cranberry sauce.
It wiggles, it jiggles.
It's shaped like a can.
It's tangy and sweet and
it's part of a plan
to make me feel silly
and quite at a loss.
It's cranberry gel;
it's *not* cranberry sauce!
Sauce is a liquid you spread on your food —
tomato sauce, gravy — whatever your mood.
Yes, sauce is a liquid you stir and you pour.
and cranberry "sauce" is a solid. What's more —
it tastes awfully good, so I guess I'll repeat it.
(It is *not* a sauce!!!) But I gladly will eat it.

Take a Poem to Lunch

I'd love to take a poem to lunch
or treat it to a wholesome brunch
of fresh cut fruit and apple crunch.
I'd spread it neatly on the cloth
beside a bowl of chicken broth
and watch a mug of root beer froth.

I'd feel the words collect the mood,
the taste and feel of tempting food
popped in the mouth and slowly chewed,
and get the smell of fresh baked bread
that sniffs inside and fills your head
with thoughts that no word ever said.

And as the words rest on the page
beside the cumin, salt and sage,
and ever slowly starts to age,
like soup that simmers as it's stirred,
ingredients get mixed and blurred
and blends in taste with every word
until the poet gets it right,
the taste and smell
and sound and sight,
the words that make it fit.
Just write.

Noah's Ark

Noah's Ark

Ancient Noah had an ark.
He filled it up by day and dark
with mammals from the local zoo.
They walked the plank up, two by two.

And also, after quite a while,
the lizard and the crocodile,
the ostrich and the spotted owl
and countless types of fancy fowl.

Too bad he also packed some worms,
some flies, some spiders and some germs,
some poison snakes and biting gnats,
(but also friendly dogs and cats).

"Hark, come aboard." He used that phrase
as people talked weird in those days.
(Though far as scholars can distinguish,
we're sure that he did not speak English.)

There is one fact that I abhor:
he did not pack one dinosaur
or tiger with a saber tooth.
He plain forgot, that is the truth.

Undercover Raccoon

The raccoon's always ready for an undercover task.

And that should be quite evident; he always wears a mask.

Some work as detectives, secret agents, double spies.

Be wary of his messages; they often will be lies.

You will not see him often as he works by stealth at night.

He plies his trade beneath the moon and sleeps by morning light.

He's furtive, yet successful. He will very seldom fail,

this undercover mammal — from his mask down to his tail.

The Hippo

I understand
that the hippo on land
is an animal lacking in grace.
His body is stout
as he lumbers about
and he looks like he's quite out of place.

But the hippo will gloat
when he jumps in to float
and you see just his eyes and his nose.
He bobs with such ease
like a cloud on the breeze.
It is where he belongs, I suppose.

Eloise

Here's the tale of Eloise
who will not say a "thank you, please."
Who loves to smack her lips and slurp,
and worse yet, break some wind and burp.
She never sits up at the table,
learned her manners in the stable.
That makes lots of sense of course,
as Eloise is just
a horse.

The Shark

The shark, a creature full of guile,
despite his constant, gaping smile,
has teeth quite sharp and pointy thin.
Be wary of his foolish grin.

If he swims near, give him a whack
or else you'll make a dandy snack.
Behind his sparkling toothy white
his mind is filled with thought of bite.

The Dogfish Really Is a Shark

Here's a fact that's plain and stark:
the dogfish really is a shark.
It has a bite, but doesn't bark.
This fact is quite incredible.

He's fond of eating other fish.
Crustaceans are a favorite dish,
and mollusks are a frequent wish,
so long as they are edible.

The dogfish likes to swim and stretch.
Though agile, it does not play catch
or ever chase a stick and fetch.
While sad, it's not quite fret-able.

If all these facts leave you agog,
remember it's not fowl nor frog.
The dogfish is more shark than dog
and therefore quite un-pet-able.

Underbite

I've never seen a sadder sight —
a beaver with an underbite.
His jaw was tight. His bite was blunt.
His lower teeth stuck out in front.
He could not do what beavers should.
His teeth just could not bite through wood.
He could not, even in a jam
help his family build a dam.

It seems that what he needs to face is
time in orthodontic braces.

Goose and Moose

It's hard to tell just what a goose
will have in common with a moose.
Or better yet, just what three geese
will have in common with three meese.
(Is that the plural for a mouse?
Is grice the plural for three grouse?)
I'll say this once, I'll say this thrice,
the plural for a moose is mice,
or plural for three mice is meeses.
I think that I may fall to pieces.
I feel my dizzy state increase
about the mice, the grice and geese.

Nervous Rex

Nervous Rex is temperamental,
strung quite tight, yet kind of gentle.
Half the size of an average horse,
his favorite place is my lap, of course.
Life dealt him a grand surprise.
He's never acted quite his size.

When Rex and I walk to the park,
he runs to hide when small dogs bark.
That's bad enough — there's more. Just that
he's frightened of our neighbor's cat.
Chicken from both ends to middle,
harsh words make my poor Rex piddle.
This creates an awful muddle —
this creates an awful puddle.

Rex would gain much vim and vigor
if he learned that he is bigger.
While this would change him in a snap,
I'd kind of miss him on my lap.
His fear makes him a dog complex.
I love him still, my Nervous Rex.

If Dogs Could Talk

If dogs could talk, what they would say
would simply take your breath away.

Like: I don't want to see your knees.

Or: Pass a bit of roast beef, please.

When dawning sun shines in the east,

they'd say: It's time for morning's feast!

When silent, still and somewhat broodish,
their minds are simply on your food dish.

Some might speak with British accent,
sniffing one another's back scent.
Some might lisp and some might stammer,
some would have atrocious grammar.
Some would chitchat, some would twaddle.
Some would rush and some would dawdle.
Curling on your soft bed nightly,

most would say: Good night

politely.

Aunt Jane's Cats

Cats are lounging on the rug,
soaking sun and feeling smug.
One is on the kitchen chair,
paws of fur up in the air.
One is stalking, with disdain,
birds outside the window pane.
Five are resting while they scan.
Two are in the litter pan.
One thing — I am certain that
Aunt Jane always loves a cat.

She takes in every wretch and stray,
cleans and feeds them, so they stay,
eat her food and rest a spell,
give her house a feline smell,
kind of stale and sour, or bitter.
In return she hears the pitter
pat of tiny padded feet.
Makes her life feel quite complete.
With her cats and telephone,
Auntie never feels alone.

The Curiosity Shop

I like the Curiosity Shop.
Its owner is a cat,
a long and lanky tabby
with a bright blue flowered hat.

The shelves are filled with marvelous things
like bright red magic beads,
Aladdin's lamp for rubbing,
and Jack-in-the-beanstalk seeds.

The great wide bins have catnip and milk.
The cupboards have no doors.
The lower shelf has puzzles.
There are toy mice on the floors.

But what of the Curiosity —
doesn't it kill the cat?
Not her, she's planning nine lives
in her bright blue flowered hat.

Snail Races

There never is a slower pace
than snails competing in a race.
On your mark, get set and go.
The one that's way ahead is slow.
The one that's far behind is slower.
Most snails are more stop than go-er.

Perhaps there are no slower tales
than races made up of such snails.

Slithery, Slidery, Scaly Old Snake

Slithery, slidery, scaly old snake,

surely your body must be a mistake.

Your eyes, mouth and tongue wisely stay on your head.

It seems that your body is all tail instead.

You gobble your dinner, you swallow it whole —

a mouse or a frog or a turtle or mole.

Ugh!

Why don't you eat ice cream or chocolatey cake!

Oh, slithery, slidery, scaly old snake.

The Elephant Has a Bad Earache

The elephant has a bad earache.
The centipede stubbed all his toes.
The giraffe has developed a nasty sore throat
and the rhino can't breathe through his nose.

The mockingbird has an unclear ache.
The lion's so hoarse he can't roar.
The hog cannot eat, as his tummy's upset,
and the parrot can't talk anymore.

The doe has a pain in the deer ache.
Just what should the beast doctor do?
The duck is so sick she can't possibly float.
It's a really bad day at the zoo.

Loony Ideas

Questions

Do dark brown cows give chocolate milk
and white cows give vanilla?
Is overfeeding baby chimps
the way zoos make gorillas?

Do small cars grow to minivans
and vans grow into trucks?
Are quackers just a funny term
for food we feed to ducks?

Do people live in our TV
and act out all the shows?
Are angels plagued with dandruff when
our streets are filled with snow?

Are clouds just puffs of shaving cream
that giants dropped while shaving?
And would these shaven giants smile
to see me down here waving?

Do babies grow in cabbage fields
with diapers on their heads?
Do farmers pluck the babies up
and make sure they're well fed?

Suppose the moon was really cheese,
right down to each round crater.
Would that mean other planets might
be rounded baked potaters?

Suppose the earth was really flat,
a wide and open ledge.
Well, if you drove your car all night
would you fall off the edge?

I have a lot of questions
about earth and time and space.
But when I get my answers,
brand new questions
take their place.

I Wish

I wish to rent a gibbon.

I wish to meet a gnome.

I wish to fly to Zanzibar, so far away from home.

I wish to ride a camel all the way to Timbuktu.

(I wouldn't even mind a nasty saddle sore or two.)

I wish to get some gossamer and fashion up some wings.

I wish,

I wish,

I wish,

I wish to do so many things.

I wish that I'd get lucky — get just one of my great wishes.

Any would be better than to stay home doing dishes.

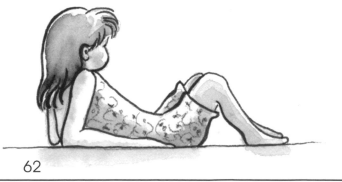

The Wild Calliope

Come hear the wild calliope
where ponies gallop wild and free.
They'll ride you to the sun and moon,
while cranking out a wistful tune.
The ponies, pink and blue and gold
are all for hire, but never sold.
So grab a ride while you are young,
shout out a bit, stick out your tongue
and hang on tight for all it's worth.
There's not a better ride on earth.

A Note to the Moth Who Ate My Sweater

I hope that you are feeling better
now that you are full of sweater.
But, frankly, don't you think it's rude
to use my clothes as common food?
I'd rather share my bread and rolls
than deal with sweaters full of holes.
The next time you intend to dine
on sweaters that are clearly mine,
I must insist — call you to task —
don't take a bite unless you ask.
By now, I think you surely know
the answer is a big, loud,
NO!

Odd Pets

They're portly and perky, my passel of pets,
the oddest that you've ever seen.
There's Chi-Chi, who's stylish and Kidney, the Red.
You've guessed it! Each pet is a bean.

There's Pico, and Pinto, and Saucy, who's baked,
there's Susan, who's black-eyed (she fights),
there's Pedro, the Mexican jumping bean, who,
so oddly, is frightened of heights.

My mother is happy as they make no mess.
They're quiet; she knows how to treat 'em.
She often comes home with a brand new supply
because sooner or later, we eat 'em.

Shampoo, Shampoo

Shampoo, shampoo,
what do you do,
up on my head like foamy glue?
I'll form you into rabbit's ears,
a witch's nose,
a monster's tears.
Light white fluff,
like puffy clouds,
a werewolf's cloak,
a vampire's shroud,
my spaniel's snout,
a fireman's hat.
I'll make my arm a baseball bat.
A pigeon's beak,
a quacker's bill.
I rinse it off;
I've had my fill.
I see the water rushing out,
as down the drain
go beak and snout.

Spinning Dry

If I had a choice, when it's time to get clean
I'd like to jump into our washing machine
for sudsing and soaking and rolling and churning
and bobbing and bubbling and twisting and turning.

Next comes my chance to feel just like a flyer
as I'd get to hop out and spin in the dryer.
I'd roll all around with a fluttering flopping,
just floating and turning with no thought of stopping.

It sounds like such fun, this incredible fling,
that I wouldn't mind if I got static cling.

The Nose

There's a lot to know about the nose,
I suppose.
It has the perfect place
on the middle of your face.
And without pause or excuse,
I will ponder on its use
or uses. There are many.

The nose's virtues number plenty.
And the first, make no mistake
about every breath you take.
The air goes in and out
through your cute prodigious snout.
Your nostrils have some hair in there
to filter out the air.
Nothing can compare, if you please,
to a loud, wet, satisfying sneeze.

If not for the nose on your face, I am told,
your head would explode when you have a cold.
If it did not protrude out in space,
then kissers would likely crash into your face.
One last use. (This may give you pause.)
When impersonating a walrus, your nose can hold straws.

My Leaky Faucet

My nose, a leaky faucet, has
a drip, drip, drip.

I wipe it so it won't land on
my lip, lip, lip.

I think that I'm allergic to
all weeds, weeds, weeds,

and long-haired cats
and vegetables
with seeds, seeds, seeds.

All winter long,
I cough a lot
from mold, mold, mold.

It's hard to say it's
different from
a cold, cold, cold.

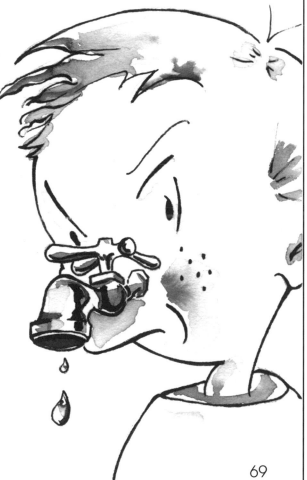

My sister just says
"Bless you, and stop,
please, please, please."

I answer with a
"Thank you," then I
sneeze, sneeze, sneeze.

The Wind Was Wild

The wind was wild, the wind was stout.

It blew my bedroom window out.

It blew my clothes around the street.

It swirled around my head and feet.

And after all was said and done,

it flew me quickly towards the sun,

up through the sky and out to space.

I felt a smile across my face.

I circled 'round the moon and then,

I headed toward the sun again,

past asteroids and space debris,

past Venus, then past Mercury.

I reached the sun and on the spot I turned around —

it was too hot!

I landed quickly in my bed.

My mother came inside and said,

"Get off that bed and clean this mess!"

Her face showed signs of pure distress.

Outside the blustery wind still blew.

Oh, if she knew. Oh, if she knew.

The Sun Just Had a Nasty Day

The sun just had a nasty day,
refused to smile or shine.
It stayed behind the dark gray clouds,
a mottled grim design.
But shortly after dinner time
one ray poked through the gray,
a spark of golden yellow warmth
reminding us of day.

If you want to please us, Sun,
(don't take this as a warning)
if you're going to pierce the clouds,
please do it in the morning.

Pillow Soft, Pillow Deep

Pillow soft, pillow deep,
take me now to deep, dark sleep.
Take me gently to the moon.
I'll be there by half past soon.
Take me round a trip to Mars,
floating past the distant stars.
Take me to another place,
safely cloaked in outer space.
Lift me up and keep me warm,
keep me from the growing storm.
Even though I'm awfully near it,
make it so I barely hear it
storming gently on my pane.
Lull me back to sleep again.
Pillow, pillow, soft and fun,
stick with me till night is done.
Stay until the sun shines high.
I'll fluff you up and say, "Good-bye."

If Dinosaurs Once More Could Roam

If dinosaurs once more could roam
and call the planet Earth their home,
their eyes would bulge, their eyes would pop.
I'd take them to the mall to shop.

(You may not know this truth at all —
no dinosaur has seen a mall.)
They just ate plants beneath the skies,
no caramel-corn, no pizza pies.

The mall is full of big surprises
like special stores for special sizes.
After all the shopping's done,
I'd take them out to have more fun.

Perhaps we'd go outside to skate.
We'd spin around till it turned late.
We'd skate beneath a lighted dome,
if dinosaurs once more could roam.

Cyclops

It's tough to be a cyclops if
you've less than grade-A vision.
You bump against your monster friends.
You can't see with precision.
It's tough to find good glasses that
won't jiggle out of place,
or make the others giggle as
they fall right off your face.
It's tough to be a cyclops, and that's where my story ends.
I think it would be easier
to get a contact lens.

(I think that I can get half-off at the mall.)

There's Something Growing in Our House

There's something growing in our house.
It's blue and quite well fed.
It's majorly disgusting.
(That is what my sister said.)

This monster in our kitchen has
not uttered yet one word.
So, if it growls or grumbles loud,
well, this we've not yet heard.

It has no form or function — not
an eye, a nose or snout.
I think it will be leaving when
our freezer is cleaned out.

Mining for a Poem

Mining for a poem,
pining to go home
to where the rhyme and meter make some sense.
Digging for a clue
for what my words should do
all safely bound within a picket fence.

Searching for a rhyme
is not a waste of time,
and rhythm must be meter's closest friend.
Together they go dancing,
lithely prancing and romancing
till the poem comes to a satisfying end.

I Work with Words

I work with words,

with ideas and rhyme.

They grow in my head when

I give them some time

to simmer, to sizzle,

to slather around.

I have stock in letters

I store by the pound.

I tweak them.

I salt them.

I eat them for snacks.

I mold them.

I ply them.

I pile them in stacks.

I stop when I'm done.

When I'm finished,

I know it.

Call me a wordsmith,

a writer, or

poet.

Counting Sheep

Four, six, eight, ten.
I'm back to counting sheep again.
Twenty, forty, sixty-eight.
I want to sleep as it's quite late.
One hundred five, one hundred six.
My mind is simply playing tricks.
Two hundred eight, two hundred nine.
I'm still awake. The sheep are fine.

They're chewing on my favorite socks.
They're sniffing at my lighted clock.
They're nuzzling by me in the sheets.
They're warming up my frozen feet,
dozing by my pillowed head,
curling up beside my bed,
cuddling up beyond my sight.
I'm drifting off . . . and so,
good night!

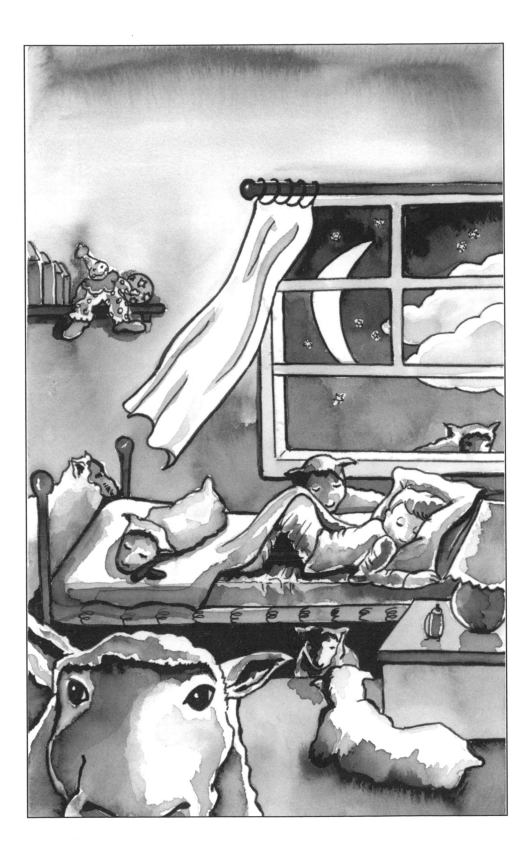

Title Index

Aunt Jane's Cats 54

Aunt Myrtle Has Geraniums 12

Betty's Room 16

Counting Sheep 78

Crack an Egg 32

Cranberry Sauce 41

Creamed Spinach Soufflé 39

Curiosity Shop, The 55

Cyclops 74

Dogfish Really is a Shark, The 49

Elephant Has a Bad Earache, The 58

Eloise 47

Famished Famella 35

Garden More than Odd, A 26

Goose and Moose 51

Grandpa Used to Shave Each Day 10

Handy Storage 37

Henry the Hatter 22

Herbert Hillbert Hubert Snod 4

Hippo, The 46

His Look Is Wild 20

I Wish 62

I Work with Words 77

If Dinosaurs Once More Could Roam 73

If Dogs Could Talk 53

Jelly, Jam, and Buttered Toast 40

Lazy Jane 15

Little Bit of Nonsense, A 2

Lucia Hemphill Todd McBean 6

Marrying Margaret 18

Matthew Brindle, Upside Down 9

Matthew McHavish 24

Melon Head 36

Mining for a Poem 76
Monster-Meat Stew 30
Moon Eggs 33
My Gramma Can't Bake Cookies 34
My Leaky Faucet 69
My Uncle Jack 5
Nervous Rex 52
Never Ask a Cow to Dine 31
Noah's Ark 44
Note to the Moth Who Ate My Sweater, A 64
Odd Pets 65
Old Woman and the Magical Sack, The 19
Nose, The 68
Pillow Soft, Pillow Deep 72
Questions 60
Rapunzel 28
Shampoo, Shampoo 66
Shark, The 48
Silly Sally 21
Slicing Salami 8
Slithery, Slidery, Scaly Old Snake 57
Snail Races 56
Spinning Dry 67
Stacking Dishes 14
Sudden Baldness 21
Sun Just Had a Nasty Day, The 71
Take a Poem to Lunch 42
Tasteful Jewelry 38
There's Something Growing in Our House 75
Underbite 50
Undercover Raccoon 45
Wild Calliope, The 63
Wind Was Wild, The 70

About the Author

The Poetry Lady, Denise Rodgers, is a professional writer and children's poet. Fortunately for children, she is unable to write any poetry that is not preposterous, ridiculous, or downright funny. Her poems have been published in *Children's Digest* and *Junior Trails*, and her work has also been included in Jack Prelutsky's *20th-Century Collection of Poetry for Children.* Her first book, *A Little Bit of Nonsense,* is illustrated by Michigan artist Julie Martin.

When she is not writing poems or visiting schools, Denise writes newspaper ads and newsletters for retailers across the country and writes features and columns for national trade publications. Denise and her husband, Peter, have two sons, Ted and David, who attend Michigan State University. They live in Huntington Woods, Michigan, with Jagger, a black-and-white English cocker spaniel.

The Poetry Lady is available for school visits and poetry work-shops. For more information, write Creative Writing Press, Inc., 3642 West Eleven Mile Road, Berkley, Michigan 48072, or call 1-800-760-6397. Or visit the author's web site at www.ThePoetryLady.com.

About the Illustrator

Julie Martin is a graphic artist who works in the corporate

world by day, and makes "kid's art" in the evening.

"Illustrating for kids is one of the most impor-

tant things I do,"

says Julie, "and

definitely the most

fun!" Julie makes her

home in Shelby Town-

ship, Michigan, with her husband, Leon. They are the

proud parents of two sons, Lee and Ross, and a little dog

named Murphy.

School Visits

Would you like to bring a lot of nonsense and fun to your school? The Poetry Lady, Denise Rodgers, is available for school visits and poetry workshops. Experience the sheer fun of word play and creativity with The Poetry Lady. Contact the publisher at (800) 760-6397, or write Creative Writing Press, Inc., 3642 West Eleven Mile Road, Berkley, Michigan 48072. Or visit the author's web site at www.ThePoetryLady.com.

Would you like another copy of

A Little Bit of Nonsense?

A perfect gift for children, teachers — anyone who loves funny poetry.

Publisher's special is $19.95/book, including shipping for the first book, and $16.90 for each additional book in the same shipment.

Name _____

Address _____

City/State/Zip _____

Phone _____

Email address _____

Please send

_____ Copies of "A Little Bit of Nonsense"
(number)

    1st book _____$19.95

    Each additional book (x $16.90 each) _____

    Total amount (please send check or credit card info) _____

CREDIT CARD PURCHASE:

Either mail this form to Creative Writing Press, Inc., 3642 West Eleven Mile Road, Berkley, MI 48072 **or fax** to 1-248-582-9223.

Card number _____

Expiration date _____

Name on card _____

Signature _____

PAYING BY CHECK?

Simply fill out the form at the top of this page and mail to Creative Writing Press, Inc., 3642 West Eleven Mile Road, Berkley, MI 48072. For more information, call 1-800-760-6397.

~ Please photocopy this page. Do not tear from book. ~

Would you like another copy of

A Little Bit of Nonsense?

A perfect gift for children, teachers — anyone who loves funny poetry.

Check out the author's web site at
www.ThePoetryLady.com

or send $19.95 (includes shipping) to

Creative Writing Press, Inc.
3642 West Eleven Mile Road
Berkley, Michigan 48072
For credit card purchase information, turn back one page.
(800) 760-6397
Fax (248) 582-9223

~ **TURN BACK ONE PAGE FOR ORDER FORM.** ~